John Smith, George Warren Barber

History of the Hermit of Erving Castle

John Smith, George Warren Barber

History of the Hermit of Erving Castle

ISBN/EAN: 9783744793162

Printed in Europe, USA, Canada, Australia, Japan

Cover: Foto ©ninafisch / pixelio.de

More available books at **www.hansebooks.com**

HISTORY

OF THE

HERMIT OF ERVING CASTLE

BY

GEORGE W. BARBER,

A STUDENT AT ANDOVER.

Written for the Hermit, at the suggestion of his numerous
visitors and friends.

ANDOVER:
PRINTED BY WARREN F. DRAPER.
1868.

THE HERMIT'S STORY.

I, JOHN SMITH, known as the Hermit of Erving Castle, was born in the city of Perth, Scotland, July 10th, 1823, and consequently am now in my forty-fifth year.

My father, Robert Smith, was a marine in the service of the crown, and so passed the greater part of his time away from his family. Indeed, I never saw my father but twice, and then he treated me with only cold neglect. My mother died when I was but an infant, and of her I have no recollections whatever. Being thus early deprived of my natural protectors, I should have been abandoned to the cold charities of the world, had not my aged grandmother, on my mother's side, had pity upon me, and taken me to her own home and heart, and cared for me until I was able to earn a livelihood. For this motherly kindness on her part I have ever felt truly grateful.

During this period I was sent to the government schools three years, free of expense — a special privilege granted to all soldiers' and orphan children. The training in these schools was excellent, and I learned to read, write, and keep accounts sufficiently well for transacting ordinary business.

OCCUPATION.

My next step was to enter into business; for when a lad has completed the regular course at these government schools, he is assisted in entering upon any trade or occupation he may desire. And each one is allowed, to give him a fair start, two suits of clothes, a pound — five dollars American gold, — for pocket-money, and five pounds for his outfit. Taking a fancy to peddling, my five pounds were invested in cheap jewelry, knives, and the like, and I started out, when about fifteen years of age, with a peddlers pack upon my back, to seek my fortune in the wide world. But as the jewelry and knives made quite a heavy burden, and required not a little polishing in damp weather, I soon tired of such wares, and as fast as I disposed of them filled my pack with dry goods. I continued in this business several years, and during that time carried my pack over a large part of my native island.

AMONG THE HIGHLANDS.

I took especial pleasure, however, in travelling among the Highlands, for as few peddlers visited that section business was not only better there than elsewhere, but the peddlers themselves received a more cordial reception. In fact, I found all strangers were welcomed to the frugal hospitality of the mountaineers; and not unfrequently, in bad weather, I spent weeks with them free of charge, so anxious were the people to see and converse with some one " from abroad." .

KEY TO MY LIFE.

It was when a young man, and following my occupation among those romantic Highlands, that an event occurred which decided my whole future. It was the meeting at one of those rustic farm-houses, nestled among the hills, a beautiful girl, whose life seemed designed for a counterpart of my own. She was a person of rare beauty, pleasing manner, and queenly bearing, who exactly filled my ideal of a woman, and captivated my heart. Being the daughter of a respectable well-to-do highland farmer, she was possessed of more than ordinary culture, and occupied a superior social position. Hence I was coy in manifesting my affection for her, supposing she was looking for some one whose wealth, occupation, and rank would compare more favorably with her own. Nevertheless, when at her father's house, she showed me many little attentions, which, under other circumstances, I should have regarded as an encouragement. For, I must tell you, as no one else will, and what few perhaps will credit when they consider my present appearance, mode of life, and aspirations, that when a young man, I was not altogether ill-favored. I dressed well and was quite fond of society. But seeing the young lady only occasionally, and being thus timid in making known my attachment, she, as she afterwards intimated, supposed me to be altogether indifferent. Considering my attitude, and desiring a home of her own, she accepted the offer of a young cattle-dealer, and eloped with him to England, or, as we say in Scotland, "ran the border." Her father pursued them into England, but it was too late. They had already married.

That first disappointment was my ruin; for I have never recovered from the shock.

When her father was made aware of my attachment for his daughter, he manifested his interest in me by offering me a home with him as long as I might choose to remain. But, as the object of my affections had become the wife of another, to avoid wounding her feelings, no less than to spare my own, I chose to flee from all those associations.

Before this disappointment I was enterprising, ambitious, doing well at my business, and cherishing bright visions of the future; but this blow broke my spirits and blasted my hopes.

I SOUGHT SECLUSION.

Despondency, like a dark cloud, now began to settle over me, leading me to renounce the world and seek retirement, that I might brood my over sadness. At

first I took secluded rooms in the city of
Edinburgh, and lived in solitude nearly a
year in the heart of that great metropolis.
But one day, while looking over a news-
paper, my eye fell upon an advertisement
for a hermit, and having read and heard
much of their retirement and quiet mode
of life, I said to myself, "That is just
what I should enjoy," so made application,
and obtained the place. For such are
the fragrant historic associations con-
nected with hermits that no lord or
noble's estate is really complete without
one ; hence they are not uncommon at
the present day in Europe.

ORIGIN OF HERMITS.

They originated about the middle of
the third century, in the idea that to
reach the highest attainments in piety

one must retire from the world to the seclusion of the cloister, and devote himself exclusively to the practice of religion. Yet in their devotion to God they did not forget their fellow-men, but were stimulated in their daily life to deeds of charity by the words of our Saviour: " Inasmuch as ye have done it unto one of the least of these my brethren, ye have done it unto me "; hence not only the way-worn and famishing traveller, but all who were destitute or afflicted were the especial objects of their pious care.

Not a few of this class have distinguished themselves in the history of the past. We read of Peter the hermit, who by his earnest preaching roused all Europe to arms, and led in person the first crusade against the infidel Turks, who, holding the city of Jerusalem, shame-

fully treated the Christians on their
pious pilgrimages to the Holy City.
History also speaks of Simon Stylites,
" who, for thirty years, preached repen-
tance to an awe-struck multitude from
the top of a pillar sixty feet high " ; and
of Benedict, who while occupying a grotto,
became famous not only as a religious
teacher and founder of schools, but also
of a celebrated order of monks.

HERMITS AND HERMITAGES.

Having given a brief sketch of the
origin of this mode of life, and cited some
instances of historical interest, we will
now speak of hermits and hermitages as
found at the present day.

If there is a natural cave upon the
lord or noble's estate, the hermit occupies it; but if not, a lodge is built for

him, usually of stone, and fitted up in a most rustic style. Here the hermit lives, supported, as are the hounds and deer, upon the nobleman's bounty, and no one is allowed to visit him without his patron's consent. The attraction of a hermitage consists chiefly in its rustic, picturesque, and pious appearance. A modest altar occupies a conspicuous place, and all the furniture is of the plainest and most primitive style. The hermit's dress, too, is simple, being usually a long cloak, tied around the neck and girt loosely about the body; and his bed consists of the skins of wild animals spread upon the floor. To make him put on as wild a look as possible he is not allowed scissors, neither knife nor razor; hence his hair, nails, and beard grow indefinitely long, oftentimes to his great inconvenience. His food consists chiefly of hermit-bread, and a few simple dishes, which he prepares for himself. He spends his time in devotion, reading the Bible and other pious books, entertaining company, and in the cultivation of flowers.

All guests, after having been shown the usual attractions of the estate, the deer, the hounds, the game, etc., visit the hermit, and not unfrequently bestow upon him substantial presents. I have received from this source alone more than a hundred dollars in a single year.

MY FIRST HERMITAGE.

I commenced my hermit life at Lovet's Castle, which takes its name from Lord Lovet, of feudal renown. This was a dark, dismal place, more fit for a dungeon than a hermitage. And besides its gloomy appearance, it was rumored that a deed of darkness had once been committed there. I discovered upon the floor in front of the altar ominous stains, which in the stillness of the night wrought upon my imagination, dispelling slumber and filling my drowsy ears with sad and mournful sounds. Yet every precaution was taken to keep the fact from me. But one day while a member of the lord's family was showing some guests over the hermitage one asked in an undertone, pointing to the spot on the floor, " Was the young man murdered here?" "Yes," was the reply; " he fell a victim here." I afterwards learned that he was a young man of fifteen, the prospective heir of the estate, who was brutally murdered by the connivance of one who expected to become possessor of the property in the

event of the young man's death. The
deed was charged upon the hermit who
was then occupant of the place, but sus-
picion finally fastened itself upon a near
relative who coveted the property, and
scrupled at no means of becoming its
possessor. I remained here about four
years; but the incumbent lord being a
Catholic, no especial friendship sprang
up between us. Eventually, Lady Hays
visited the castle, and, learning that I
was a Protestant, said she had a Catholic
hermit, and asked if I would be willing
to change places with him. I gladly accepted the proposal, and soon removed to

BLACK-HEATH HERMITAGE,

under the patronage of that estimable
lady. This place was not only peculiarly
attractive, but all its surroundings most

congenial. As good Lady Hays was widely known, and her society coveted by all, visitors constantly thronged her mansion, who were especially kind to me.

After having spent six years very pleasantly at her hermitage she determined on a tour of Eastern travel, and I accepted an invitation to act the hermit's part in some theatrical plays, then about to be brought upon the stage in the city of Inverness. Here I spent one season as an actor, but did not enjoy that heartless, bustling life.

It was while acting in Inverness that an incident occurred which may serve to illustrate the reverence with which hermits are regarded by all the lower classes of Europe. Indeed, this reverence sometimes amounts to superstition. The event to which I have referred took place

2

late one night, while I was on my way home from the evening's entertainment. Being tired with my walk and the evening's duties, I stopped in an old barn to rest, and finally concluding that I would remain until morning, I lay down in a corner upon the hay.

ENCOUNTER WITH THE GYPSIES.

Soon some marauding gypsies came in and struck a light. I feigned sleep, thinking perhaps I should be unnoticed; but they soon observed me, and examining me closely discovered upon my finger a heavy gold ring. Then said one in a whispered tone: "Let us chop off his finger, and get that ring"; but the other — not being in favor of doing things by halves, suggested a still more radical measure—said, "No; let us cut his throat."

Upon this I opened my eyes, and, rising up, asked what they wished. They, recognizing me, exclaimed, "Oh, it is the hermit!" and from their superstitious reverence for this class of persons, gave me no further cause for alarm.

LORD FIEF'S HERMITAGE.

While engaged in the plays, Lord Fief, who was a regular attendant at the theatre, learning that I was then without a home, gave me an invitation to enter his hermitage, which I gladly accepted. But I did not enjoy life there, as I received but little attention, being often neglected for a whole week. Hence I not unfrequently suffered for the necessaries of life. During the two years I remained there I became acquainted with Lord McDugald, of the Isles to the north of Scotland, and desiring to visit that part of the country, he urged me to become his hermit. I did so, and remained with him more than six years, receiving every attention a hermit could desire.

KENMORE CASTLE.

But thinking the cold climate did not agree with me, I gladly complied with the wish of the Marquis Breadalbane, of Kenmore Castle, — whose wife, the amiable Lady Kenmore, was of the same persuasion as myself, a Baptist, — and removed to his hermitage, situated in a more congenial part of my native island. I remained here until his decease, a period of about three years, passing the time pleasantly.

Being again without a permanent abode, Lady McDonald, of Keppeth Castle, offered to make me her gardener and give me a home for life, if I would renounce my faith and become a Catholic. But I told the good lady that my religion was dearer to me than a hermitage, and that I would sooner be like Him who had " not where to lay his head," than violate my conscience in so vital a matter ; hence took my departure.

WHY I CAME TO AMERICA.

While lamenting the loss of a home I chanced to fall in with several young men who were soon coming to America, and one said to me, " Why break your heart about an old hermitage ? the woods are filled with caves in America ; come, go with us, and you will find a home." This was an argument which, under the circumstances, I could not resist, and as the steamer was to leave in a few days I engaged passage, and soon found myself under way to the New World.

A TERRIFIC STORM ARISES.

We had been out but a short time when a storm arose, which continued to increase for several days, until the rigging was swept away and much other damage done to the steamer. For three days we were all hatched below, and suffered much for the want of pure air and fresh water. Once a heavy sea striking the side of the vessel burst in the port, and swept me unceremoniously out of my berth upon the floor. At times waves swept over the deck, and we thought the vessel was sinking. Many realizing the powerlessness of human aid, besought Him who calmed the stormy lake with the words,

" Peace ; be still," to interpose in our behalf ; but it was my prayer that if our bodies found a watery grave our souls might reach that blest haven of rest — heaven.

THE STORY OF JONAH.

Under these most trying circumstances I remembered the story of Jonah, who fleeing from duty was confronted by a violent tempest, and I could not but feel that this storm was a judgment upon me for murmuring at my lot, and fleeing from my native land. Many times I wished that we might turn back, or that I might be landed upon any shore Christian or Heathen. But as this was impossible, I made a solemn vow that if the Lord would pardon my ingratitude and save my life I would never again murmur

or complain at my lot. Let no one think
I am exaggerating, for the storm was so
terrific that two vessels pursuing the
same course with us were lost. But a
day or two before we reached New York
the weather became fine again, and all
was gayety upon the steamer's deck; but
I blessed the Lord with heartfelt gratitude
that I was not in the depths of the sea,
nor in the belly of a whale; yet such
was my fearful experience on that voyage
that I never intend to venture on the
ocean again.

FIRST YEAR IN AMERICA.

I arrived in New York in the spring
of 1866, and spent part of the first season
in gardening about the city, but the heat
was so oppressive that I could not endure
it. Accordingly, having acquaintances

in Boston, I went there, and spent the first winter in doing any little jobs which I could find. Yet I could not have supported myself during the cold weather, had I not previously laid by a little money for a rainy day. But not liking life in the city, I began to cast about me for some employment which would prove congenial.

Being told that I could make a tidy living by picking berries in the vicinity of Shutesbury, Leverett, and Lock's Pond and selling them in Boston, and thinking this employment would give me an opportunity of being much in the country, I determined to go there and prospect. I found blue-berries in abundance, and saw that when the season for them had passed there would be a plenty of huckle-berries, so I immediately commenced picking.

HOW I SUPPORTED MYSELF.

When I had gathered as many as I could conveniently carry, I started with them on my back for Boston. To prevent crushing the berries I put them in boxes, and tying them up in an old shawl I threw them upon my back like a pack. I usually carried about twenty quarts at a time, which, as I gathered only the largest and nicest berries, I always readily sold on reaching the city. I generally disposed of them at twenty or twenty-five cents per quart, thus realizing as the proceeds of the trip some five dollars. It usually required about three and a half days to go from Leverett to Boston, a distance of eighty-five miles, and the same to return. I always felt a little tired after this long walk, and so did not return immediately, but spent a day or two in visiting the Public Garden, for there I had an opportunity to gratify my great admiration for flowers. Thus I was usually gone from home nine or ten days. In these jaunts I carried my provisions, consisting chiefly of crackers, and my coffee-pot also with me. When meal-time came I had only to stop by the way, like a soldier, boil my coffee, and eat my food. I also carried my bed-rug, and usually stopped at night in an old house, barn, or shed, wherever night overtook me, but was careful to be up and off in the morning before people in general were stirring. One school-teacher man-ifested her kindness by allowing me to stop in the school-house over night when-ever I passed that way. Here I not only found a stove upon which I could heat my coffee, but also a warm place in which to sleep when the nights were chilly.

I may add in summary, that it usually took me two days to gather the berries, and another to sell them, after reaching the city; seven days were consumed in travelling; thus ten days were occupied in preparation for and accomplishment of one of these journeys, and for all this the account stood as follows:

20 quarts of berries at 25 cts.	5.00
Expenses in the city,	1.00
Net proceeds	4.00

I confess it was rather discouraging, ten days' hard work for four dollars; yet with my simple mode of life, that little sum would stand me in stead for several weeks.

CHESTNUTS AND WREATHS.

After the berry season had passed I gathered chestnuts, and when the chestnuts were gone I made evergreen wreaths, which I also carried in the same way to Boston. I could take along thirty or forty wreaths at a time, for which I received as many cents apiece, hence realized from ten to fifteen dollars a trip. This was much better than I did with the berries or chestnuts. My appearance, with this strange-looking pack upon my back, excited not a little wonder and merriment in the towns through which I passed ; but my occupation was at least an honest one, and why should I mind what people said or thought.

I have often been asked why I did not take the cars, which ran so, near, when

I went to market with my berries. My ready answer to such an inquiry is, that the net proceeds of the trip would have been consumed in going one way, for the fare to Boston is nearly four dollars. And what then? Why in that case there would have been nothing for me to do but to trudge back home, with a purse as empty as when I started.

While picking berries in Leverett and vicinity, I made my home at a cave in that town, but as it afforded me but little protection in rainy weather, I often passed the night in a school-house not far distant.

HOW I DISCOVERED MY PRESENT CAVE.

Late in autumn while picking chest-nuts, I discovered the cave which I now occupy; but having taken considerable pains to make my former abode comfortable, I decided to winter there. In the following spring, March 1867, I removed to this place, and for fear of being discovered and driven away kept myself secluded, seldom leaving my cave, and then avoiding as far as possible all intercourse with men. Nor did I trade at the stores in Erving, but went to the adjoining towns for my coffee, sugar, and meal, being careful not to enter the same store twice, for fear of attracting notice, or of being questioned as to my home. When in the vicinity of my cave I avoided the road as much as possible, going through woods and fields, out of sight of human habitations. I dwelt alone in these deep solitudes until late in the following autumn, and no mortal knew that I tenanted these rocky fastnesses. That summer I spent here alone — no,

not alone — was the happiest of my life.
During those months, as I reviewed the
past, my heart was filled with thankful-
ness to the kind Providence which had
guided me here, and often from the altar
of my heart and the cliffs of these rocks,
there ascended the incense of devotion.
In those hours of deep reflection, the only
thought which disturbed my tranquility
in this secluded spot, was the **fear of**
being discovered, and driven away from
the place which had now become so dear
to me.   But time passed rapidly on, and
ere long the forest leaves began to rattle
beneath my feet, and soon the ground
was whitened with the early snows; I
accordingly commenced to gather in
wood and make other preparations for
the inclemency of winter.

HOW I WAS DISCOVERED.

One day I climbed upon the ledge, and nailed a few boards upon a tree to break the cold winds which blew down upon me through the crevices of the rocks. Having accomplished my object I threw the stone which I had used for my hammer carelessly down into the bushes in front of my cave. No sooner had it reached the earth, than some one near where it disappeared cried out "Halloo!" I made a like reply, and jumped down quickly to see who the intruder was. My first thought on hearing this voice was, "I am discovered, and this is the sheriff who has come to arrest me or turn me out into the snow;" but on getting down so that I could see a distance into the woods, I caught just a

3

glimpse of a man running from me as fast as he could. I then said to myself, " He has now certainly gone for the officers of the law, and I shall soon be a prisoner."

DARK FOREBODINGS.

It was then near the first of December, and a dark day for me, for I thought all my fond anticipations were now at an end. And I said, " What shall I do if I am driven away from my dear cave? Where can I go? What can I do to support myself through the long cold winter? If I am taken before a magistrate and fined for trespass I shall certainly be sent to jail, for I have but a little money." Oh, those long, sad hours of fear and anxiety! While pondering these dark forebodings my fire burned low, and I watched the dying embers on the hearth, imagining that I read in them my own sad end. Thinking the sheriffs would soon make their appearance, I did not replenish my fire, but sat through the weary hours of the day and far into the night expecting every moment to see officers of the law stalking up the little footpath which led to the door of my secluded home. I not unfrequently imagined that I heard the noise of voices, and the crackle of breaking limbs echoing through the woods. After nightfall I thought I caught through the trees occasional glimpses of an approaching light. At length fatigued with long watching and almost benumbed with cold, I wrapped my scanty clothing about me, and laying down upon my bed of straw passed a restless night, thinking and dreaming of the woes which I thought were in store for me. And during the reflections of those long hours I asked myself, again and again, shall I flee at the dawn of morning, like a guilty wretch, and leave my home and little hard-earned store of provisions, and all that I have?" "No," I answered; "I am not guilty of wronging any one, and I will not flee, but will meet the consequences, whatever they may be, like an honest man, here, where I have lived and enjoyed so much. The scene of my happy life shall also be the scene of my calamity." The following day was the Sabbath, the first of December, 1867, and I arose at the first flush of dawn, and, shivering with cold, anxiously watched, through the tedious hours of another day, the little footpath which led down into

the woods; but saw no one. At last
night came, and I consoled myself with
the thought, that the man whom I saw
was only a straggler, like myself, as fearful of me as I was of him, and that I
need feel no more concern about being
arrested. So the next morning I again
built my fire, and my heart and cave
were once more radiant with the sun-
shine of hope. Now thinking that all
my dangers were only imaginary, I was
as much exhilarated with joy as I had
been previously cast down with fear, so
went about my accustomed work singing
more cheerfully than before. But im-
agine my surprise at discerning, about
the middle of the forenoon, three men
cautiously approaching, and apparently
seeking my dwelling. Instantly the
thought flashed across my mind, " These

are the dreaded officers"; and I was tremulous with fear. On their nearer approach, I discovered that they were armed with axes and spades, —

SINGULAR WEAPONS FOR MAGISTRATES.

"What," thought I, "are they going to chop me in pieces, and bury me here? If this is to be my lot, oh that my ashes might repose in the cave which has so long been my happy home." After discovering me, they approached, with an inquisitive look and hesitating step. When they had come within speaking distance I inquired, "Who are you?" They replied "We were building a road through the woods, so thought we would come up and pay you a short visit." They then asked, "Who are you?" I replied, "I have recently come from. Scotland,

and having no home or friends in this country, I have taken up my abode in these rocks." After these mutual explanations all fears vanished, and I invited them to come into the cave and sit down. One of the three was Mr. Death, who saw me on the previous Saturday, and of whom I caught occasional glimpses as he beat a hasty retreat through the woods.

WHAT LED TO MY DISCOVERY.

He, narrating how he chanced to find me, said: "I was at work in the woods, and discovering many fresh tracks in the newly-fallen snow, thought I would see whither they led. So following them, I soon found myself in front of a very strange-looking place. The mouth of the rock was nearly filled with wood, over which poured a volume of smoke, darkening the cliff as it rolled and eddied upwards. Upon the rocks near by I saw a most singular-looking object, with long hair and matted beard, and I said, ' Is this a wild man of the woods, or have I come upon the retreat of robbers and highwaymen?' And being not a little frightened, I turned and fled, lest I should be pursued, and perhaps murdered." I told them that I, too, had been in agony ever since I saw the man, thinking an officer of the law would soon be put upon my track. But they frankly told me that no one in this community could wish to injure me, and that the owner of the land would probably have no objections to my remaining, if I did not cut down the growing trees for wood. This intelligence was not only highly gratifying to me, but removed many fears.

VISITORS POUR IN UPON ME.

The next day a company of ladies paid me a visit, bringing with them for my comfort, no small quantity of delicacies and substantial provisions. This was unmistakable evidence that I was in a friendly and kindly disposed community, when I had supposed all were unsympathizing, and perhaps hostile. My joy at this unexpected revelation well-nigh overcame me. Nor was this all; but each day brought new evidence of the interest which the community felt in me; for visitors now began to throng my cave, many of them bringing eatables and other expressions of good-will. And they continue to come from far and near; and I often wonder what attraction they find here.

Eventually the owner of the soil, Mr. Barton Wright, Esq., of Springfield, paid me a visit. He expressed much interest in me, and kindly assured me that I might live here as long as I choose. And not only this, but he gave me permission to build a road for the accommodation of my visitors, and also allowed me the privilege of picking up all the wood I might need. I now felt that the prayer so often offered, that I might be allowed to remain in this cave was answered, and my heart was filled anew with praise and thanksgiving. It seemed to me then, and does so still, that a kind Providence directed me to America, and provided for me this home. And I cannot but cherish the hope that here I may be allowed to spend the remainder of my days. Such is my attachment for this place, that I would not exchange this rude cave for a princely mansion. For the sublimity of these rocks not only reminds me of the romantic Highlands of my native Scotland, but my own spirit is in harmony with these deep solitudes. Indeed I think no lord in his castle or king in his palace happier than I.

LOCATION OF THE HERMITAGE.

The hermitage is located in the midst of a forest, of some four hundred acres, lying about a mile and a half northwest of the village of Erving. The cave itself is situated at the foot of an immense wall of granite, facing the south, which rises by broken steps as it recedes, until it terminates in a mountain of rock, reminding one of the couplet,

" Hills peep o'er hills,
And Alps on Alps arise."

ROMANTIC SCENERY

Hence the scenery around is indeed wild and picturesque. From some of these cliffs, through openings in the trees, one catches occasional glimpses of Miller's sparkling river, winding its way through the narrow valley, to add its tribute to the beautiful Connecticut. The puffing locomotive, speeding the lightning train, can also be distinctly seen, for the distance of several miles, following its iron path along the river's bank, while its shrill whistle wakes the woods in echoes, which are reverberated by the granite sounding-board, back of the hermitage. The dense woods come to the very mouth of the cave, and scattering trees spring out of fissures in the rock on either side and above the entrance. In fact a venerable chestnut has planted its roots firmly within a crevice of the floor-rock of the cave itself, and bends its ponderous trunk to lift its proud head to the skies.

PULPIT ROCK.

A few feet to the left of the entrance a shelving rock projects several feet beyond the main wall, which has received the name of Pulpit Rock. It is nearly level on the top, and forms a good platform for a public address. Religious services were held here for the first time Sunday, April 26th, 1868, by George W. Barber, a student at Andover Theological Seminary, who discoursed upon the " Parable of the Talents," to an audience which had come together for that purpose. I may also add, it is hoped that such services will not be of unfrequent occurrence here.

MOSES' ROCK.

A few feet to the east of Pulpit Rock, a perennial fountain of pure water gushes out of a crevice in the rock. This I discovered soon after finding the cave, and exclaimed, "Here is where Moses smote the rock, and the water gushed out." And I then said to myself, "Surely this cave, with this beautiful spring so near at hand, must have been designed for some homeless one; and why not for me? for does not he who said 'not even a sparrow falls to the ground without my notice,' care for his own children? Certainly there can be no harm in my dwelling here, if no other mortal knows of it or wishes it for his home."

THE RABBIT'S CLAIM.

But after having taken formal possession of the cave, I found it occupied by
one who held it not only by right of
discovery, but also by right of actual
possession. For one evening after I had
retired for the night, a formidable rabbit
stalked in, and made himself quite at
home. But soon discovering an intruder,
he fixed his indignant eyes upon me, as
much as to say, What business have you
here, sir? but not fearing especially the
rabbit clan, and thinking the cave large
enough for us both, I determined to remain until morning; the rabbit at length
despairing of looking me out of countenance, and fearing the issue of a pitched
battle, calmed his troubled spirit; and
betook himself to a corner, and preparing

his couch, retired for the night. The
next morning he manifested not a little
irritation, as he watched my domestic
operations from a crannie of the rocks.
But finding me unmoved by his pugna-
cious demonstrations, and not being un-
reasonable in my demands, he doubtless
concluded that discretion was the better
part of valor. Accordingly, when his
tempest of passion had fully subsided, he
came back to the cave, and we eventually
became mutual friends, and cheered not
a little each others loneliness. Like
too many other people, however, my
rabbit partner had a very inquisitive
nature, which he not unfrequently ex-
hibited in meddling with matters that
did not at all concern him. For often,
when I was away from home, he would
poke his nose into and upset things which

were exclusively my own. I frequently took him to task for this, and tried many expedients to cure him of his bad manners. But his inquisitive disposition had so grown with his growth and strengthened with his strength, that all attempts to correct it proved fruitless. One evening, on returning to our abode, I did not find him at home, as he was quite fond of company; but soon discovered that he had been up to his old tricks. Being tired, I soon turned in for the night, feeling not a little vexed at his conduct in my absence; and I said to myself, " I will pay you for this." But while meditating on some mode of revenge, I heard his familiar rustle among the leaves, and knew that he would soon come up the ledge; so catching up the fragment of a board, I struck it down upon the

4

rocks, to frighten him as he came in; but, as it was quite dark, I chanced to hit the rabbit himself a severe blow upon the head, which prostrated him senseless to the earth, and caused his death soon afterwards. I was very sorry for what I had done, having no intention of injuring him. However, as he was now dead, I thought I might appropriate, without any charge of cannibalism, that flesh which had been so largely fattened on meal furtively taken from my chest. Accordingly I dressed and cooked him, and bade him adieu in the soup pan.

MY MOUSE FRISKY.

In a short time I noticed that even the rabbit's claim to the cave was not absolute, but was shared with a mouse, who kept house in a corner, from which

a crevice extended to apartments below,
where he betook himself in all times of
danger. But the mouse soon learning
that I was no enemy, grew very familiar,
and I became much attached to him.
Indeed, he was company for me, and
afforded me not a little amusement; for
he would sit upon my knee, leap upon
my shoulder, and eat from my hand.
He came every morning regularly for
his breakfast, and if his wants were fully
supplied, would never interfere with my
provisions; but if neglected, was sure
to forage whatever he could find. He
delighted in his activity, and would per-
form many acrobatic feats, such as leap-
ing, turning somersets, and the like,
which would have been a credit to any
gymnast. Not unfrequently when visitors were present, he would give an

exhibition of his sprightliness, much to
:eir amusement and wonder. On account of his activity and sportiveness, I
gave him the name Frisky, which he soon
learned, so that he would come at call.

MY BIRDS.

Last summer a little bird built its nest
in the mouth of the cave, where, though
not unfrequently enveloped in the curl-
ing smoke, it laid four spotted eggs, and
reared as many beautiful young. I took
especial pleasure, not only in watching
the building of the tiny nest, and observ-
ing the patient waiting of the mother
bird for the eggs to break forth into life,
but also in noting the parental solicitude
for the callow brood, until they could
care for themselves. These, too, became
quite intimate, and depended largely

upon me for support. Nor were these all the animated beings which cheered and enlivened my solitary abode.

THE SQUIRRELS.

It was not long before I discovered a family of four striped squirrels, living a little way up the rocks, who eventually became very neighborly. But I soon learned that when they ran in of an afternoon, their visit was more of a beggar's errand than a friendly call. These, too, became so fearless that they would come and take their pittance from my hand. But the squirrels, as well as the birds and Frisky, have either been frightened away or devoured by

ROBINNIE, THE CAT,

who is now my only pet, and prides herself upon being mistress of the hermitage.

She was brought here by a lady, who, being about to leave town, begged that I would adopt her. Not having a heart to turn her houseless away, I took her into the bosom of my family, and gave her a home by my hearthstone. As she is pleasant company, and seeks most of her living in the woods, I have become strongly attached to her, and could not now consent to part with her. When successful in her hunting excursions, however hungry, she brings her prey to the hermitage, and seeks to attract my attention before devouring it. And when her appetite is appeased she takes special pleasure, as her loud purr indicates, in getting upon my knee for an approving and doting caress. She is a good mouser, and a special terror to all mischievous creatures that prey upon the hermitage.

THE CAVE ITSELF.

The dimensions of the cave are some twelve feet in length and breadth by ten in height, in front, with the roof-stone sloping back, until it reaches nearly to the floor-rock. Thus the shape of the cave, together with the base-rock, is quite irregular; but I have changed it for the better not a little, since entering it, and I hope to improve it still more. Thus far I have used neither powder nor wedge in breaking the rock in pieces; but my plan is to keep my open fire in one place on the rock until it becomes hot, and then by dashing water upon it cause the surface suddenly to cool and crack in pieces. The bank wall in front of the cave is constructed largely of stones, which I have in this way broken in pieces and removed from the interior. But there is much still remaining on the top and sides not within reach of the fire, which I intend to remove by blasting. I hope before another winter to fill the front of the cave (which is now rudely boarded up) with logs, and to stop the crevices with moss, which will not only make my ·rock-dwelling as warm as a house, but also give it an antique and picturesque appearance.

MY FURNITURE.

My furniture, which has recently been increased by contributions from visitors, now consists of two or three dilapidated chairs, and an old straw mattrass, upon which I sleep, spread upon the granite floor. Two or three rusty cans, a coffee pot, together with a few plates, knives, saucers, etc., constitute my crockery and cooking utensils. These are kept on my dresser, under the shelving edge of a rock just outside of the cave.

MY FOOD.

This consists chiefly of stirabout — Indian pudding, — of which I am exceedingly fond, and which I eat without milk or sauce. Occasionally I bake a loaf of hermit-bread which is much esteemed in all hermitages. I use no meat or fish, except occasionally when I buy a few herrings, or obtain a little wild meat; neither do I use butter or any groceries, except a little tea or coffee. But I am fond of fruit and vegetables, and always use them when obtainable. Last year I raised a few hills of potatoes here and there in sunny places among the rocks about my cave. But this year I have already planted more potatoes, onions, lettuce, and the like, which I hope will yield me many a delicious meal. .I enjoy my simple diet, and keep healthy and robust upon it, having never been sick in my life.

Thus far the narrative has proceeded in strict accordance with the facts as given by the hermit himself. The spirit and style of the narrator, as originally dictated, have also been preserved as far as possible.

That which follows has been added by the writer, thinking it would be of interest to the reader to learn something further respecting the appearance and character of our singular friend.

ADDITIONAL FACTS.

Since it became known that a hermit had made a cave among these rocks his home, the land upon which it is situated has advanced considerably in value, and it promises to be a place of so much attraction, when it becomes more widely known, that several enterprising gentlemen have expressed their desire to purchase some of these rocky acres, with a view of erecting a public house. .

We would venture the suggestion that when the land is disposed of a chance be given the present tenant of the rocks to secure a title to a few acres of the adjoining soil. If this can be accomplished he proposes to cut down a portion of the trees, and by the diligent hand of cultivation make the wilderness to bud and blossom as the rose.

APPEARANCE, ETC.

The hermit is a man of about medium size, and of light complexion. A heavy beard covers his face, but his head is somewhat bald. His countenance and eyes indicate intelligence, and are free from all marks of sensuality or intemperance, though he acknowledges that he was once intoxicated, under the following circumstances: Soon after being discovered, some young men paid him a visit, bringing with them what they called "cider." Being invited, he drank with them, yet soon found that he had been deceived. But on coming to himself once more, he resolved never again to touch, taste, or handle that which "at the last biteth like a serpent and stingeth like an adder."

He has kept his resolve, and now when invited to press the drunkard's cup to his lips replies, "I have joined the tee-totalers." He has often been urged to open a dram-shop at his cave, being assured that he would have "plenty of customers," and could make enough money in a short time to buy what land he desires. But he says, "Not a drop shall be sold here with my consent; nor do I covet the company of those who are addicted to its use."

Furthermore, he does not use tobacco, and says, "I am not going to sell it, for my cave smokes enough now for me; and I do not wish to make it any more disagreeable to ladies and others by the presence of tobacco fumes."

HABITS.

He rises early, usually with the sun, and soon prepares his morning meal. And after putting his cave in order for the day, he busies himself, when not engaged in gardening, in knitting stockings, which he does with considerable facility. He says he knows it seems very simple to see a man knitting in this country, but in Scotland the men when not employed out of doors do this chimney-corner work as much as the women. He sells the stockings to his visitors, and in this way gets money enough to support himself in his primitive and simple mode of life. On pleasant days he may not unfrequently be seen sitting at the door of his cave, humming some pious tune while plying his needles, with his cat seated cosily upon his knee.

SOCIABILITY.

It might perhaps be inferred from his love of solitude, that he would be taciturn and distant; but, on the contrary, he uses elegant language, and is more than ordinarily social. When drawn out in conversation he is free to narrate the incidents of his own life, or to speak of the manners and customs of the Scotch. He communicates much interesting information, not only of the lords and nobles under whose patronage he has lived, but also relative to the brave and unconquerable Highlanders, among whom he has extensively travelled. He is a man of considerable general intelligence and good breeding, which he has unconsciously acquired from contact with the nobility of his native land.

NEITHER A KNAVE NOR A SIMPLETON.

In fact our hermit is not, as many have supposed, a knave or simpleton, but an honest, intelligent, Christian man, and by persuasion an open communion Baptist.

His library is not extensive, but well-chosen, consisting of, at present, a Bible and hymn-book, of which he makes daily use. As might be inferred he is a lover of music, and when requested entertains his visitors with hymns, or songs of an elevated character. But it is contrary to his idea of propriety to sing songs on the Sabbath. His favorite tunes are Balerma, Old Hundred, Jerusalem, Comfort, and the like, which he sings with the spirit and understanding also.

FROM THE ATHOLE PAPER.

" John the Hermit. — It is inscribed in Holy Writ ' that it is not good for man to be alone '; although this fact is an outbreathing of Deity, yet many of human kind have, at various times and places, and from all kinds of religious, moral, and pecuniary reasons, tried hard to gainsay it, and by their actual life endeavored to demonstrate the many charms of solitude that lie hidden in cloister and hermitage.

" For instance, we have among the craggy cliffs of our neighboring town of Erving a hermit who fain would establish among our granite rocks and limpid streams a *facsimile* of the hermitages of Albion and Scotia. ...

" Among the vast domains of England's nobility it is customary to have a romantic spot inhabited by a hermit, with long disheveled hair, matted beard, and finger-nails like the talons of an eagle, who daily adds additional charms to render the surroundings more and more picturesque. This is the desire of our John, and explains our statement of his being a hermit by profession. ...

"He is, without doubt, very industrious in his mountain home; the spring, the rock, the ledges, the garden spot of potatoes, springing onions, and flowers in bloom, testify to his love of industry, and his appreciation of the beautiful in nature. He has been largely visited from all the neighboring towns, and seems while employed in his knitting to recall with pleasure the kindnesses of his numerous visitors. ...

"The hermitage is within easy distance of the Erving House, kept by mine host Trask, where guides can be procured and the best of fare, and courteous attention, both going to and returning from Erving Castle.

"The scenery from the crags around is indeed romantic, and will in itself repay a visit. We would say to our readers, go and see Erving Castle."

AN UNWELCOME VISITOR.

Among his many visitors he has had one who was not particularly agreeable. This was a suspiciously-acting fellow, who, while secreting himself in the woods, chanced to discover the hermit's habitation, and entering unbidden, not only abused the hermit much, with insulting language, but also threatened to turn him out of his cave. He boasted of having been a rebel soldier, and seemed perfectly reckless, giving the solitary dweller much occasion to fear ; yet he finally went away without doing him any harm. The hermit afterwards learned that his visitor was a fugitive from justice, stained with dark crimes, and that even while he was at the cave abusing him detectives were watching for the criminal on the other side of the mountain. But he has not since visited the hermitage, and the hermit hopes he will not again.

ALL ARE WELCOME.

The hermitage is open, and it is a pleasure for the hermit to entertain company every day except the Sabbath. His visitors may occupy a seat in the hermitage, drink at Moses's Rock, climb the cliffs, or wander through the forest at their pleasure. Come one and all who wish to see a *bona fide* hermit — one who has lived a secluded life for nearly twenty years, and covets no other.

LOCATION.

Erving is situated on the Vermont and Massachusetts Railroad, extending from Fitchburg to Greenfield, and some ten miles from the latter place. Persons wishing to visit the hermit can leave the cars at Erving, and there obtain directions. The hermitage is about two miles distant, but a passable carriage road has been opened nearly to the place.